headshell

written by
pete ✦ wentz
&
hannah ✦ klein

illustrated by
lisa ✦ sterle

special thanks:
sally ✦ cantirino
layouts 1-25

VAULT COMICS PRESENTS

DYING INSIDE

A HEADSHELL PRODUCTION

WARNING

THIS BOOK INCLUDES DISCUSSION OF SUICIDE AND DEPICTION OF SELF-HARM. WHILE WE HOPE THIS BOOK WILL HELP SOME READERS FEEL LESS ALONE, ITS CONTENT MAY BE TRIGGERING. PLEASE ONLY READ AHEAD IF YOU ARE SAFE AND SUPPORTED. IF YOU ARE STRUGGLING, IT'S IMPORTANT TO SHARE YOUR FEELINGS.

THE SUICIDE & CRISIS LIFELINE IS 988.

FOR INFORMATION ABOUT FOREIGN OR MULTIMEDIA RIGHTS, CONTACT: RIGHTS@VAULTCOMICS.COM

FEATURING

Daisy Grenade

"LEFT FOR DEAD"

SCAN TO PULL THE PIN & LISTEN

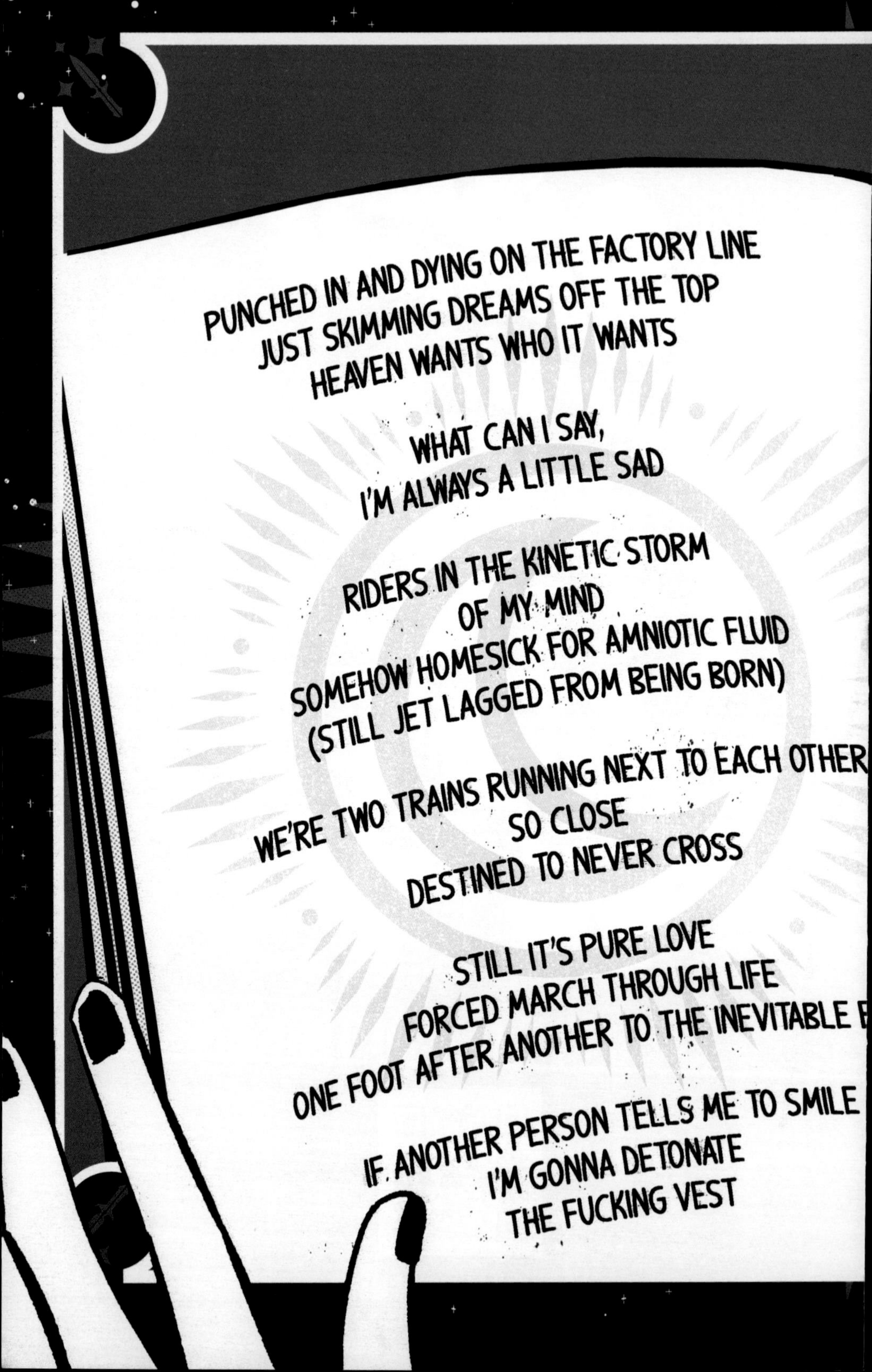

PUNCHED IN AND DYING ON THE FACTORY LINE
JUST SKIMMING DREAMS OFF THE TOP
HEAVEN WANTS WHO IT WANTS

WHAT CAN I SAY,
I'M ALWAYS A LITTLE SAD

RIDERS IN THE KINETIC STORM
OF MY MIND
SOMEHOW HOMESICK FOR AMNIOTIC FLUID
(STILL JET LAGGED FROM BEING BORN)

WE'RE TWO TRAINS RUNNING NEXT TO EACH OTHER
SO CLOSE
DESTINED TO NEVER CROSS

STILL IT'S PURE LOVE
FORCED MARCH THROUGH LIFE
ONE FOOT AFTER ANOTHER TO THE INEVITABLE E

IF ANOTHER PERSON TELLS ME TO SMILE
I'M GONNA DETONATE
THE FUCKING VEST

I JUST NEED YOU TO LOVE ME
MORE THAN THEY HATE US

AXE TO MY PSYCHE
I SWEAR
REPEL DOWN THE FROZEN SHATTER
TO THE ICE CAVE AT THE BOTTOM
UNDERGROUND THE PRESSURE TURNING US
FROM COAL INTO DIAMONDS
AND BACK INTO COAL AGAIN

REMEMBER
WHEN TIME WAS STILL
ON OUR SIDE

ASH

THIS IS PERFECT.
"PARTING IS SUCH SWEET SORROW."
PSYCH.

自殺サークル
BURN YOUR FIRE
FOR

OCTOBER
RIP Elliott
RIP ME
TODAY IS ELLIOTT SMITH'S *DEATH DAY.* AND SO, IT SHALL ALSO BE *MINE.* BECAUSE I'M MAKING IT THAT WAY. OBVIOUSLY.
NOW, BEFORE I GET INTO THE WHOLE *WHY* OF IT ALL, I FEEL I SHOULD EXPLAIN THE LORE OF *ELLIOTT SMITH* TO THOSE OF YOU WHO MAYBE AREN'T FAMILIAR WITH OUR EMO KING.
SCREEEEE
ORIGINAL WOODEN FLOORS, ASH!

SORRY, MOM!
I SWEAR TO GOD, ORIGINAL WOODEN FLOORS IN BROOKLYN ARE TREATED LIKE HOLY SCRIPTURES. ANYWAY...
THIS IS ELLIOTT SMITH.
UGH!
SHRIMPS, YOU'RE LITERALLY THE LOVE OF MY LIFE, BUT NOT EVERY LASER POINTER IS FOR YOU.

PAVEMENT
ELLIOTT SMITH IS AN ICON AND ALSO HAPPENS TO BE MY FAVORITE MUSICIAN.
MY FAVORITE. MUSICIAN.

NOT ONLY IS HIS MUSIC ABSOLUTELY SEMINAL, BUT WE HAVE A LOT IN COMMON. FOR EXAMPLE, WE BOTH LOVE DRUGS.
IT'S JUST MY ANTI-DEPRESSANT.
NO, IT'S NOT.
MOM, CHILL. IT'S JUST CBD!
NO, IT IS NOT.
Hhaak
Hak Hhaak

YOU'RE ONLY ALLOWED TO WORK HERE UNDERAGE BECAUSE YOU'RE MY NIECE. IF THAT'S ALCOHOL, YOU'RE FIRED.
OBVIOUSLY, IT'S SPRITE!

YOU GET THE POINT.
I would kill for some god damn noise
OH, FUCK. I LOVE THIS SONG.
I would kill but a girls' got poise
I would kill to be one of the boys
I would kill I would kill

CANDY
WE'RE ALSO BOTH ARTISTS.
OK, HE'S AN ARTIST.
EVANGELION
I AM A LYRICIST WITHOUT A BAND. ABSOLUTELY WORTHLESS.
WHICH BRINGS ME TO MY NEXT POINT.

I HATE MYSELF AND I WANT TO DIE. THAT'S THE OTHER THING ELLIOTT AND I HAVE IN COMMON. AND I KNOW WHAT YOU'RE THINKING.
MOTHER FUCK--OWW!
KLANG
LANGUAGE!
SORRY.
HMMPH--

ANYWAYS, I KNOW WHAT YOU'RE THINKING.
"NOOOO, YOU HAVE SO MUCH TO LIVE FOR. WHY WOULD YOU DO THIS? YOU'RE ONLY SIXTEEN. THINGS WILL GET BETTER!"
THE TRUTH OF THE MATTER IS... I'M CHRONICALLY DEPRESSED AND TIRED.
TIRED OF THE LOWS.
TIRED OF THE DOCTORS.
TIRED OF THE MEDS.

IT'S A LOT OF WORK TO BE THIS SAD! PLUS, THE EARTH IS GOING TO EXPLODE SOON ANYWAY-- LOOK!
IT'S LITERALLY SNOWING IN OCTOBER.
DROSE
BUT YESTERDAY I WAS SWEATING IN SHORTS!
YOU DO THE MATH.

SO, I'M GOING TO KILL MYSELF. TONIGHT. JUST LIKE ELLIOTT DID, BUT WITHOUT ANY WITNESSES OR SIGNIFICANT OTHERS AROUND. I'M NOT IN THE BUSINESS OF FRAMING PEOPLE FOR MURDER.
NOT THAT I EVEN COULD-- BECAUSE I CAN'T EVEN GET A BOYFRIEND TO WATCH ME KILL MYSELF.
I DID GET THIS COOL-ASS KNIFE FOR IT, THOUGH--
OH, BY THE WAY, ELLIOTT STABBED HIMSELF. THAT'S HOW HE DIED. I DON'T THINK I TOLD YOU THAT YET.

AHA! THERE SHE IS.
ISN'T SHE PRETTY? I GOT HER OFF GETSY.
AND NOW I'M GOING TO STAB MYSELF WITH HER.
THINGS ARE ABOUT TO GET GORY--SO TRIGGER WARNING TO SKIP A FEW PAGES IF YOU ARE SQUEAMISH ABOUT BLOOD AND GUTS.

Now Playing
Needle in the Hay
Elliott Smith
MY YEAR OF RE
NECRONO
NAKED LU
SHADE THE CHA
UZUMA
HERE WE GO.
MROW
WHOOPS. SORRY, SHRIMPS. YOU DON'T NEED TO SEE THIS.

OK--FOR REAL THIS TIME. HERE WE GO.
HOW DID HE DO THIS WITHOUT HESITATION WOUNDS?

NEW PLAN.
KRRK KRRK
KRRK
DROOOOP
THAT OUGHTA DO IT.

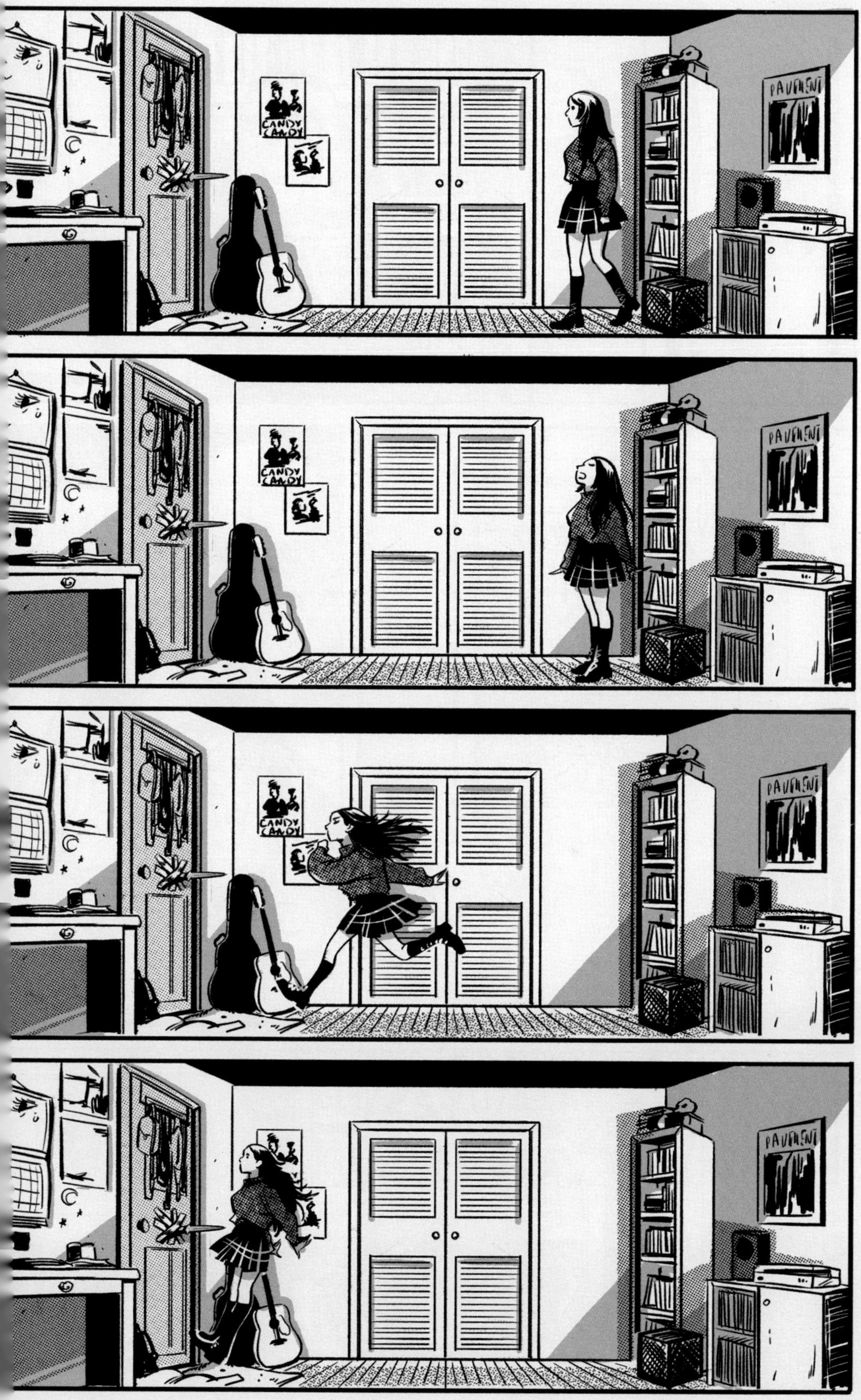
CANDY CANDY
PAVEMENT

WHAT IS WRONG WITH ME?
ASH! GREG IS HERE FOR DINNER!
GREG IS MY MOM'S BOYFRIEND. I HATE THAT GUY.
HURRY UP!
OK, YEAH-- I'D RATHER LITERALLY DIE THAN HAVE DINNER WITH GREG.

OH.
PSYCHO

DID IT WORK?
UH, THIS SHOULD HURT, RIGHT?
THE WOUND ISN'T EVEN AS BIG AS THE KNIFE.

AM I IN HEAVEN OR SOMETHING?
ASH! SERIOUSLY! COME DOWN NOW!
OH, GOD. I'M IN *HELL.*
WAIT, JEWS DON'T BELIEVE IN HELL. SO ARE WE ALL WRONG? THAT'S TEA.
ARE YOU COMING?

PAVEMENT
WHAT THE HELL DID YOU SPILL ON YOUR FLOOR?
BLOOD.
OK, WELL, CAN YOU TAKE A BREAK FROM YOUR SATANIC RITUAL TO COME HAVE DINNER?

YES, I WILL COME DOWN FOR... DINNER.
GREAT.
...
WHAT THE *FUCK* JUST HAPPENED?

STOMP
STOMP
SIGH

AREN'T YOU GOING TO SAY HI TO GREG?
HI, DOCTOR GREG.
IT'S JUST GREG. YOU CAN DROP THE "DOCTOR"--ESPECIALLY WHEN YOU'RE USING MY FIRST NAME AND YOUR DELIVERY IS DRIPPING WITH SARCASM.

GREG IS A *PSYCHOPHARMACOLOGIST* AND SAYS HE LOVES HELPING PEOPLE, BUT I'M CONVINCED HE JUST LOVES PLAYING GOD.
I THINK I CAN HELP HER. HER MEDS ARE JUST OFF.
I DON'T FEEL COMFORTABLE TESTING ON HER.
HE IS OBSESSED WITH THIS NEW DRUG CALLED *SOMNIA* AND HAS BEEN PUSHING IT ON *EVERYONE*. IT'S LIKE HE'S GETTING A CUT OR SOMETHING.
SORRY, *GREG*. CAN YOU PASS THE FRIED RICE?
I DON'T TRUST HIM. ALSO, HE HIGHKEY SUCKS.

IT'S NOT THE CLASSIC "I DON'T LIKE ANYONE MY MOM LIKES" THING.
MOM'S BEEN GRIEVING FOR EIGHT YEARS NOW. I WANT HER TO FIND LOVE.
Glare
JUST NOT WITH HIM.
Shiver
SHOP
I'M GOING TO MY ROOM.
CRASH

OK, HONEY. I LOVE YOU.
MAKE GOOD CHOICES.
WHAT THE FUCK IS THAT SUPPOSED TO MEAN? HE'S WEIRD, RIGHT?
OK, TIME TO GET BACK TO WHAT'S ACTUALLY IMPORTANT--A-K-A THE MAGICAL FUCKERY GOING ON.
SLAM

AND IT ALL STARTS WITH HER.
I NORMALLY DON'T DO THIS, BUT I THINK I HAVE TO...

LODGE A COMPLAINT.

Getsy
TRASH
MARK UNREAD
MARK READ
ARCHIVE
help with order #54688652
Dear GetsyWitch2006,
I am writing to let you know that the knife you sent me is not usable for the purposes needed. Unfortunately, you sent me a fucked up magical totem of sorts, which, while may be cool to some, isn't super helpful to me. Please let me know how to proceed, as I no longer want this object in my home, but I also would like compensation. I'm sorry if I'm being a total bitch, I can't even believe I'm writing a complaint right now, but this just happens to be super important. Please let me know ASAP what to do. Sorry again for complaining. Maybe I should've known a knife from "GETSY-WITCH2006" would have magical properties, but to be fair, witch culture is very mainstream at this point, so I thought maybe you were just being cute, or maybe you're a witch but don't sell magical objects without a WARNING. Anyway. Thanks. Ash.

ow to proceed, as I h
also would like
l bitch, I can't even
but this just happens to
P what to do. Sorry ag
a knife from "GETSY-
es, but to be fair, witch
I thought maybe you
tch but don't sell magi
nks. Ash.
SEND
GETSYWITCH2006: OMG I AM SO SORRY! I PROMISE I HAVE AN EXPLANATION! So basically
BLAH. BLAH.
BLAH BLAH.
BLAH BLAH BLAH.
BLAH. BLAH.
We both live in Brooklyn so if you want to meet up, I'd be happy to fix this for you.

NORMALLY, THERE'S NO WAY IN HELL YOU'D FIND ME MEETING UP WITH A STRANGER WHO DEALS KNIVES FOR A LIVING. BUT...IF SHE CAN MANAGE TO KILL ME, THAT'S THE BEST CASE SCENARIO.
THE ROYAL TENENBAUMS
XO
XO
THE R
"GREAT, WHERE SHOULD I MEET YOU?"

MEOW.
WELCOME TO *BUBBLES!* WHAT CAN I GET FOR YOU?
JESUS CHRIST. SHE'S LIKE A LIVING ANIME CHARACTER.

ACTUALLY, I'M HERE WAITING FOR SOMEONE. HAVE YOU SEEN--
O-M-G, ARE YOU *DYINGINSIDE22*? I'M *GETSYWITCH2006!* WELL, MY REAL NAME IS *LIV!*
ASH--NICE TO MEET YOU.
YOU ARE LIKE SO PRETTY. SERIOUSLY, WOW.
SHOULD I GET OUT OF HERE BEFORE SHE WEARS MY SKIN?

OPEN
GULP
TOO LATE.
TOO LATE FOR WHAT?
NOTHING.

WOW, THIS IS... REALLY GREAT CUSTOMER SERVICE.
I PRIDE MYSELF ON MY CUSTOMER SERVICE. I REALLY, REALLY CARE. AND I AM SO SORRY ABOUT THE MIX UP. MAY I ASK WHAT'S WRONG WITH YOUR ITEM?
CERTAINLY.
AHHHHHHHH!

PHEW.
BLEH.
OK, SO, LIKE...IT DOESN'T WORK IN THE CLASSIC WAY IT SHOULD?
EXACTLY.
YOU COULD'VE USED THIS TEACAKE AS AN EXAMPLE, YOU KNOW. BLOOD IS REALLY HARD TO GET OFF VEGAN SHAG UPHOLSTERY.

ALTHOUGH... IT SEEMS TO WORK FINE HERE.
IF I WAS IN THE BUSINESS OF THROWING TEA PARTIES, YES, IT WOULD BE CONSIDERED WORKING.
UM. WELL. WHAT KIND OF BUSINESS ARE YOU IN EXACTLY?
THE BUSINESS OF DYING.
YOU'RE A MURDERER?? AREN'T YOU LIKE...MY AGE?

DON'T WORRY, I'M NOT A MURDERER.
I'M JUST CHRONICALLY DEPRESSED. YOU CAN SIT BACK DOWN. I'M NOT GONNA HURT ANYONE BUT MYSELF.
YOU'RE GOING TO HURT YOURSELF?
WELL, I WAS. BUT YOU'VE MADE THAT IMPOSSIBLE. BECAUSE I'M SOMEHOW IMMORTAL. AND I HAVE A FEELING THAT YOUR SUPER PRETTY GLOWY KNIFE HAD SOMETHING TO DO WITH IT.
OH. WELL, HOW DO YOU KNOW IT'S NOT JUST THIS KNIFE THAT WON'T HURT YOU?
HAND ME THAT BIG FORK OVER THERE.
OK.
WAIT! NO! I DON'T TRUST YOU, AND I DON'T HAVE A TIDE PEN ON ME.
OK, WELL, TRUST ME ON THIS--I TRIED EVERY SHARP INSTRUMENT I OWNED BEFORE DARING TO MAKE A CUSTOMER COMPLAINT. NOTHING LASTS, I HEAL UP.
OH. THAT'S... SOMETHING.

"OH"? ANYTHING ELSE YOU WANT TO ADD?
OK, SO... DON'T BE MAD. BUT THERE HAS BEEN A BIT OF A MIXUP LATELY.
IT'S JUST THAT...I LIKE TO SEND POSITIVE VIBES TO MY CUSTOMERS, SO I PUT GOOD LUCK SPELLS ON EVERY ITEM I SEND OUT.
OK...

BUT I'M A BEGINNER WITCH, AND SO, TECHNICALLY, THERE'S LIKE DO'S AND DON'T'S OF WHAT I'M SUPPOSED TO BE TRYING...YOU KNOW, SPELL-WISE. BUT ONE DAY I WAS ON REDDIT AND I SAW THIS SUPER COOL PROTECTION SPELL--
YOU'RE GETTING YOUR SPELLS FROM REDDIT?
IT'S ACTUALLY A REALLY USEFUL DATABASE, YOU WOULDN'T BELIEVE THE--
JUST GET TO THE POINT.

SO, LIKE, MAYBE THE PROTECTION SPELL WAS, UM...MORE INTENSE THAN I THOUGHT?
NO SHIT.
I AM SO SORRY. OBVIOUSLY, I WILL HELP YOU FIX THIS.
OH, YOU'LL "FIX THIS"? WITH WHAT, YOUR WITCH REDDIT PAGE? THIS IS MY LIFE WE'RE TALKING ABOUT. OR RATHER, MY DEATH. BUT STILL! WHAT THE HELL, LIV, THIS IS HELLA IRRESPONSIBLE!

I KNOW!
I KNOW. I REALLY FUCKED UP.
ALTHOUGH...
MAYBE THIS IS KIND OF...A *MIRACLE*?
OH, MY *GOD*, GIVE ME A *FUCKING* BREAK.

WELL, CLEARLY, IT WASN'T YOUR TIME TO...GO.
OK, BUT YOU'VE MADE IT SO IT WILL NEVER BE MY TIME TO GO. THIS ISN'T TWILIGHT, LIV! I DON'T WANT TO REPEAT HIGH SCHOOL OVER AND OVER AGAIN! I'M GOING TO LOSE MY FUCKING MIND!
OK, OK, OK. WE'RE GOING TO FIGURE IT OUT. IT'S OK.
HOW THE FUCK ARE YOU GOING TO FIGURE IT OUT? YOU'RE SIXTEEN AND DO YOUR SPELL WORK THROUGH A FUCKING SUBREDDIT!

I HAVE ACCESS TO REAL WITCHES, TOO--ELDER ONES. YOU'LL SEE! WE WILL FIX THIS. IT'S GOING TO BE OK.
SOB
I PROMISE I'LL FIX THIS.
OK.
ON ONE CONDITION...

NOW YOUR CUSTOMER SERVICE COMES WITH CONDITIONS?
IF--NO...**ONCE** I FIGURE OUT HOW TO UNDO THE WHOLE IMMORTALITY THING, YOU HAVE TO GIVE ME THIRTY DAYS.
WHAT IS THIS--SOME SORT OF TROLL TOLL SITUATION? THIRTY DAYS OF LABOR?
THIRTY DAYS OF NOT KILLING YOURSELF AND SEEING IF THERE'S ANOTHER OPTION.
SHE'S DREAMING.

DEAL.

GREAT. SO WHAT'S THE FIRST STEP?
WELL, I HAVE TO GET HELP FROM MY ELDER WITCHES...BUT THEIR SPIRITUAL SHOP IS CLOSED UNTIL TOMORROW.
SORRY.
YOU'D THINK BEING OPEN LATE COMES WITH THE TERRITORY.
IT'S FINE. I HAVE A SHIFT, ANYWAY.

YOU HAVE A JOB AT NIGHT? A NIGHT JOB?
YEAH, I WORK AT JEFFERSON HALL.
CREW
JEFFERSON HALL, THE *VENUE?* ARE KIDS ALLOWED TO WORK THERE?
MY UNCLE OWNS IT. I HELP OUT FOR EXTRA CASH AND FREE SHOWS.
WHO'S PLAYING TONIGHT?
DAISY GRENADE.
I THOUGHT THAT SHOW WAS 18+...
IT IS.

PLEASE.
PLEASE.
PLEASE.
PLEASE.
PLEASE.
PLEASE.

I'M GOING TO BE *WORKING*, SO JUST--STAY COOL, ENJOY THE SHOW.
I WILL BE TOTALLY COOL... BUT ALSO CAN WE MEET THE BAND?
CREW
SIR?
BECAUSE I'M LIKE TOTALLY OBSESSED--
OH, SORRY. UH, WE'RE HERE.
MAYBE YOU SHOULD GO TAKE A NAP OR SOMETHING.
STAY SAFE.

DEPRESSIVE EPISODE

THIS IS MY LEAST FAVORITE SHOW
SOMEBODY CHANGE THE CHANNEL IN MY HEAD

ASH, YOU'RE SO LATE.
I KNOW. THERE WAS AN... EMERGENCY.
THERE REALLY WAS!
THIS IS YOUR FRIEND, ASH?
WE'RE NEW FRIENDS!
CREW
WELL, THAT'S NICE AND...UNEXPECTED. MAYBE YOU CAN HELP HER AT THE MERCH TABLE AFTER THE SET. BE GOOD.
WE WILL!

I WENT DOWNTOWN, AND YOU TOLD ME NOT TO STAY TOO LONG
I CUT YOU SLACK
YOU BROKE MY BACK
CREW
DAISY GRENADE
CAN YOU GO MAN THE MERCH TABLE? THEIR SET IS ABOUT TO END--I JUST HAVE TO PEE.

HEY, ARE YOU OK? DO YOU NEED SOME WATER OR SOMETHING?
CREW
DO YOU NEED ANY MEDICAL HELP? I'M ASH. WHAT'S YOUR NAME?
CREW
EMMA. AND I'M OK... MY PSYCH JUST PUT ME ON A NEW MEDICATION... AND IT HAS...WEIRD SIDE EFFECTS.
CREW
BEEN THERE.

WELL, I'VE BEEN ON EVERY MEDICATION UNDER THE SUN, SO MAYBE I CAN HELP. WHAT IS IT?
SOMNIA? HAVE YOU HEARD OF IT?
REW
YOU'VE GOTTA BE KIDDING ME.
THERE YOU ARE! DUDE, THE SHOW IS ABOUT TO END, AND THEY'RE PLAYING YOUR FAVORITE SONG. LET'S GO.
...THANKS.

DAISY'S GRENADE
HI! CAN I GET THE BABY TEE IN A MEDIUM?
IT'LL BE $25. HOW IS YOUR FRIEND FEELING BY THE WAY? UH... EMMA?
CREW
OH, SHE'S FINE. SHE JUST LEFT BECAUSE HER CURFEW IS MIDNIGHT.
SHE'S SAFE TO GET HOME? IS SOMEONE WITH HER?
CREW
CA-CHING

SHE'LL BE FINE. IT'S JUST LIKE TWO STOPS ON THE L FOR HER. NO BIG DEAL.
CREW
EVERYTHING ALRIGHT?
I'M NOT FEELING WELL--CAN YOU TAKE OVER?
SURE THING, KIDDO. FEEL BETTER AND GET HOME SAFE.
IS EVERYTHING OK?
CAN WE TAKE THE L BACK?

I DON'T MIND UBERING US BACK--IT'S LATE. PLUS YOU'RE NOT FEELING WELL.
THAT'S THE GIRL.
WHAT GIRL? WHAT DID I MISS?
SHE WAS REALLY SICK AT THE VENUE FROM THIS MEDICATION THAT MY MOM'S BOYFRIEND IS ALWAYS PAWNING OFF.
"YOUR MOM'S BOYFRIEND IS A DOCTOR?"
"A QUACK PSYCHIATRIST. NOT ONE OF THE GOOD ONES."

ZZZZZZZ
HEY, EMMA--
EMMA!
ASH, DON'T--!
SCHSCHSCHSCHSCH
HSCHSCHSCH

IT'S FINE. THERE'S THAT LITTLE...*INDENT* FOR TIMES LIKE THIS, REMEMBER?
IT'S LIKE SUBWAY 101.
I THOUGHT YOU WERE DEAD!
THINK ABOUT WHAT YOU JUST SAID.
OH, RIGHT.
WE'RE GOING TO THE HOSPITAL.

VRRR
BOOP
DING
OH! IT'S TIME TO BE REAL.
IT LOOKS LIKE YOUR HEART RATE IS EXTREMELY LOW. DO YOU HAVE ANY CONDITIONS THAT AREN'T DOCUMENTED IN YOUR FILES?
I'LL TELL YOU WHAT'S WRONG WITH HER!

SHE'S ON *SOMNIA.* WHICH I'M SURE YOU HAVEN'T HEARD OF BUT--
THIS IS THE THIRD CASE I'VE SEEN THIS WEEK. EMMA, WHY ISN'T THAT PRESCRIPTION WRITTEN IN YOUR FILES?
SO YOU KNOW ABOUT THIS? AND YOU KNOW IT'S DANGEROUS? WHAT THE HELL, DUDE?
IT'S NOT NECESSARILY DANGEROUS. IT'S JUST RECENTLY BEEN FDA APPROVED, AND THE PRESCRIPTION GUIDELINES ARE A BIT...RELAXED.
BUT, EMMA, I HIGHLY RECOMMEND YOU SWITCH YOUR REGIMEN BECAUSE THIS COULD DEFINITELY BE A REACTION TO THE MEDICATION.

THIS IS MY UBER. THANK YOU AGAIN. SERIOUSLY.
Emergenc
AND YOU'RE GONNA CALL MY PSYCH, RIGHT?
YES, DEFINITELY.
OK, KEEP ME POSTED.
SORRY, RANDOM, BUT YOUR DOCTOR'S NAME ISN'T GREG, IS IT?
HOW DID YOU KNOW THAT?
I'M WORRIED ABOUT *HIPAA*--AM I ALLOWED TO SAY ANYTHING?
THNK
SHE'S A PSYCHIC, IS ALL!

I'M A *PSYCHIC?*
I WAS THINKING ON MY FEET.
SO... YOU REALLY HATE YOUR STEP-DAD, HUH?
HE'S NOT MY STEP-DAD. HE'S MY MOM'S BOYFRIEND. AND, *YES.*
GROCERY
BESIDES PEDDLING THIS WEIRD DRUG, WHAT ELSE DOES HE DO?
I'D TELL YOU, BUT WE'RE HERE. THIS IS ME.

WHAT'S WRONG?
NOTHING--
THEN WHY ARE YOU PRETENDING YOUR NAILS ARE DORITOS?
OH MY GOD-- THIS COLOR IS **GORGEOUS.** WHAT IS IT?

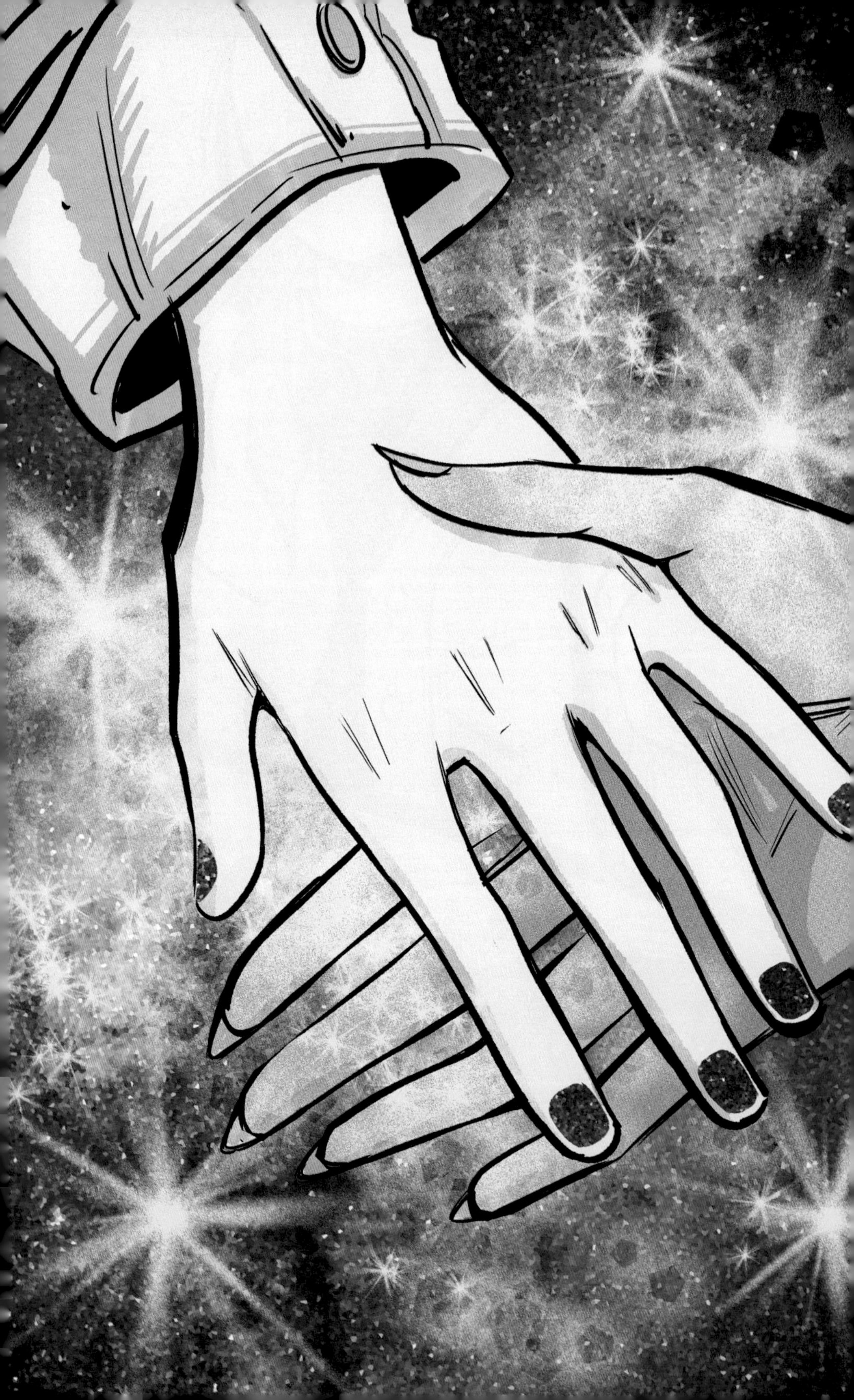

OH, IT'S--UM, IT'S CALLED "BLUE ME AWAY," I THINK? I'VE BEEN USING IT FOREVER.
YOU'LL HAVE TO LET ME BORROW IT SOMETIME. IT'S SO PRETTY.
IT IS, HUH? I GUESS I FORGOT.
SEE YOU TOMORROW AT REALM SPACE! DON'T BE LATE! WITCHES HATE THAT.
OOO, A WITCHY RULE? SPOOOOKY!
WHY DO THEY HATE IT?
BECAUSE IT'S RUDE.
OH.

HMMM.
REALMSPACE
HIIIII!
HMPF SOMEONE'S HAD THEIR COFFEE ALREADY.
OH, I DON'T DRINK COFFEE. IT'S ICKY.
REALM

KNOCK
KNOCK
KNOCK
DID YOU TELL THEM WE WERE COMING?
COME IN.
OKAAAAYYYY...

HMM.

WELCOME.

SO GOOD TO SEE YOU, LIVVY! SORRY ABOUT THE SMOKE--MORNING CLEANSE.
ASH, MEET MY WITCH MENTOR, DYLAN.
SO NICE TO MEET YOU. THANK YOU FOR HELPING ME OUT OF THIS CURSE.
CURSE?
RIGHT, YEAH-- SO I DIDN'T GIVE DYLAN THE FULL RUN DOWN YET. CAN I JUST BORROW YOU FOR A SECOND?

YOU **WHAT?!**
IT WAS AN ACCIDENT!
OOOO, SHE'S IN ***TROUBLE.***

OK, SO, LIV FILLED ME IN, AND THE GOOD NEWS IS...
...THERE'S AN EASY WAY TO UNDO WHAT SHE'S...DONE TO YOU.
YES!
THIS SHOULD DO IT.

THANK YOU SO MUCH-- YOU HAVE NO IDEA.
DON'T *EVER* DO THIS AGAIN. OK?
ALRIGHT, GET OUTTA HERE. WE HAVE TO OPEN.
BYE, DYLAN!

OK, THAT SEEMS GOOD.
SHRIMPS, YOU ALREADY HAVE NINE LIVES-- THIS ONE IS FOR ME.
OK... DONE.
VOILA!
ALL I NEED TO DO NOW IS WRITE DOWN MY INTENTION, FOLD IT UP, AND PUT IT UNDER MY PILLOW. I'LL BE FIXED BY MORNING.

CANDY
PSYCHO
KNOCK
KNOCK
KNOCK
IT'S YOUR MOM!
AND GREG!
CAN WE COME IN?
WE JUST WANTED TO SAY GOODNIGHT.
...GOODNIGHT.

YOU OK, HON? YOU LOOK... FLUSTERED. ARE YOU SICK?
I CAN'T EVEN GET SICK ANYMORE... I DON'T THINK.
I'M FINE, JUST TIRED.
HAVE YOU BEEN TAKING THE VITAMIN C PILLS I GAVE YOU?
OF COURSE...
NOT.

GOODNIGHT, BABY. SLEEP WELL.
NIGHT.
WHY IS HE STARING AT IT LIKE THAT?
NICE ALTAR.
CANDY CANDY
HE'S SUCH A FREAK.

...TOMORROW I WILL WAKE UP MORTAL...

IT'S MORNING!

DON'T FREAK OUT-- I'M NOT KILLING MYSELF. I'M JUST MAKING SURE IT WORKED.
YAY!

WHYYYYYYYYYY?

ASH! NO SCREAMING BEFORE 8AM!
DROSE
HMMPH--
HEY--IT DIDN'T WORK--PERIOD. WHAT THE ACTUAL FUCK--QUESTION MARK. ANGRY EMOJI--SEND.
boop
hey it didn't work. what the actual fuck?
are you sure you did it right?
"ARE YOU SURE YOU DID IT RIGHT? :("
OBVIOUSLY I DID IT RIGHT--I'VE NEVER BEEN MORE SURE OF ANYTHING IN MY ENTIRE LIFE--PERIOD. CRY FACE EMOJI--CAN YOU CALL DYLAN--QUESTION MARK--I NEED YOU TO COME HERE AND FIX THIS--SEND.

YOU'RE REALLY OBSESSED WITH THIS GUY, HUH?
"THIS GUY"? YOU MEAN ELLIOT SMITH?
WHO IS HE?
"WHO IS HE"? AN ICON. A GENIUS. ONE OF THE BEST SONGWRITERS OF OUR TIME. FATEFULLY POETIC. I'LL PUT HIS SELF-TITLED RECORD. ON--YOU'RE GOING TO LOVE IT.
I'VE NEVER HEARD OF HIM.
WELL, HE DIED BEFORE WE WERE BORN. HE TOOK HIS OWN LIFE WHEN HE WAS 34. IT WAS AWFUL.
THAT'S TRAGIC.
OR...IS LIFE THE TRAGEDY, YOU KNOW?
NO, IT'S DEFINITELY DEATH THAT'S THE TRAGEDY.
YOU JUST DON'T GET IT.

IS THAT WHY YOU WANT TO KILL YOURSELF? BECAUSE HE DID?
OBVIOUSLY NOT--THAT WOULD BE RIDICULOUS.
BUT YOU WERE INSPIRED BY HIM, RIGHT? I MEAN, YOU TRIED THE SAME WAY HE DID.
SURE, AS AN HOMAGE. I MEAN, IT WAS A PRETTY METAL WAY TO GO.
YOU CANNOT TELL ME YOU THINK HIS BEST WORK WAS DYING?
I DON'T WANT TO TALK ABOUT THIS ANYMORE. HE'S A GENIUS, OK? THAT'S ALL YOU NEED TO KNOW.
YEAH, AND IT WOULD'VE BEEN NICE TO GET ANOTHER FIFTY YEARS OF WORK OUT OF HIM, DON'T YOU THINK?
Elliott Smith
THIS IS HIS BIOGRAPHY? CAN I BORROW IT?
Elliott Smith
SURE, I'VE READ IT A MILLION TIMES. WHAT'S NEXT ON THE AGENDA?

SO, ALL THESE SPELL BOOKS...
NOBODY THOUGHT TO PUT THIS ON A SERVER YET?
YOU'RE THE ONE WHO GOT MAD AT ME FOR USING REDDIT.

HEY! NO SLEEPING UNTIL WE HAVE THIS FIGURED OUT.

PLOP
PLOP
PLOP
YAAAWNNN.
SORRY. THE CONSTANT ELLIOTT SMITH ISN'T EXACTLY HYPING ME UP.

CRICKET
CRICKET

The
ENENBAUMS
ZZZZZZ
ZZZZZ

YOU GUYS HAVE BEEN PULLING SOME LATE NIGHTS, HUH?
SCHOOL PROJECT.
IT'S SUMMER.
SUMMER SCHOOL PROJECT.
YOU DON'T GO TO THE SAME SCHOOL.
YOU'RE JEWISH.
OH MY GOD, CAN YOU STOP WITH THE THIRD DEGREE? JESUS.
WE HAVE A SHIFT AT JEFFERSON.
BE GOOD!
WE WILL!

DROSE
FIRST
FRANCIS BACON BAND
ENJOY THE SHOW!
WHATCHA DOIN', BEAUTIFUL MIND?
NOTHING.
DOESN'T LOOK LIKE NOTHING. YOU LOOK HAPPY. DID YOU BREAK GROUND ON SOMETHING?
HEY--
WHAT THE FUCK?

AHEM
SORRY ABOUT THAT! ENJOY THE SHOW!
IS THAT ALEX G?
WHERE?
GOT YA!

ASH, IT'S NOT FUNNY. GIVE IT BACK.
WILL YOU RELAX? WHAT COULD IT POSSIBLY BE?
WHAT IS THIS?
WHERE'S THE REAL BOOK?

October 15
I know how to undo the curse, but I
can't bring myself to tell her. I love her so
much and I don't want to lose her. I wish
had a therapist.
I still haven't told her.
I feel so guilty.
Ash ~~made~~ me
all her favorite
and we listened
The lyrics were
YOU KNEW THIS WHOLE TIME?

CAN I GET THE PINK SHIRT?
SURE! WHAT SIZE?
LARGE, PLEASE!
SUN
RCH
WHAT THE FUCK?
YOU DON'T WANT TO GET CAUGHT IN THIS CROSSFIRE.

IT'S NOT WHAT YOU THINK.
IT SEEMS LIKE YOU KEPT THE SOLUTION FROM ME BECAUSE YOU DIDN'T WANT TO LOSE ME.
WELL. YES. BECAUSE I LOVE YOU.
AW, REALLY?
YES, OF COURSE. I WAS JUST LOOKING OUT FOR YOU.

I GET IT. I LOVE YOU, TOO. COME HERE.
REALLY?
OCH
NO!

AHHHHHHH!!
OOPH--

IF YOU LOVED ME...!
...YOU WOULD HELP ME.

OK! I GET IT! WAIT! DON'T--

I WANTED TO PROTECT YOU! YOU'RE MY BEST FRIEND!
BEST FRIENDS?!
DON'T KEEP SECRETS.

WELL! IF YOU WERE BETTER AT COMMUNICATING I WOULDN'T HAVE HAD TO! BUT ALL YOU CARE ABOUT IS YOURSELF!
ENOUGH!

I THOUGHT YOU TWO WERE BEST FRIENDS.
WE ARE!
WE'RE NOT.

FOR LEASE
I had tender feelings that you made hard
But it's your heart, not mine, that's scarred

Incorporating water into cleansing
12 Help beginners love spell?
Modern Witch Tarot
Have I been cursed?
50 Be your best possible you
Rituals for the New Moon
4 Maiden, Mother, Crone
Gift ideas for a witch newbie?
So when I go home, I'll be happy to go
You're just somebody that I used to know

Sorry we're
CLOSED
32
A
Ash
don't text me.

KNOCK KNOCK
COME IN!
HI, LOVEBUG.
UM... WHAT'S UP?
JUST CHECKING IN. YOU'VE BEEN QUIET AGAIN LATELY.
EVERYTHING OK?

EVERYTHING'S GREAT--JUST LOST MY SUPPOSED BEST FRIEND, I STILL WANT TO DIE, AND I STILL CAN'T.
I'M FINE.
I HAVEN'T SEEN LIV HERE IN A WHILE. SHE WAS GOOD FOR YOU, BUG. WHY DON'T YOU GIVE HER A CALL?
NO, THANKS.
I'M SURE SHE MISSES YOU, TOO.

I DON'T MISS HER.

Everything reminds me of her.
ARE YOU KIDDING ME?
I'M SO SORRY. LET ME FIX IT!

WHAT-- SO YOU CAN LIE SOME MORE? GO AWAY.
I'M SO SORRY FOR EVERYTHING! I WAS BEING SELFISH! PLEASE LET ME MAKE IT UP TO YOU. I KNOW IT MUST BE HARD TRYING TO DO IT YOURSELF!
LIV, WE WERE JUST TALKING ABOUT YOU.
REALLY?
WOULD YOU LIKE TO COME IN?
YES!
NO!

THANK YOU.
WELL, YOU GIRLS LET ME KNOW IF YOU NEED ANYTHING.
...
LIV, ASH HAS REALLY MISSED YOU--
MOM!
YOU MISSED ME?
NO.
TINK TINK TINK
LISTEN, I'M REALLY SORRY. SERIOUSLY. YOU WIN.
YOU DON'T HAVE TO HYPNOTIZE ME. I WANT TO HELP YOU. ALSO, THAT ISN'T A REAL HYPNOSIS TECHNIQUE.
THAT'S NOT WHAT THE INTERNET SAYS.
TINK TIN-

HAVEN'T WE LEARNED THAT THE INTERNET IS OFTEN WRONG WHEN IT COMES TO MATTERS OF MAGIC AND THE UNKNOWN?
...TRUE.
IT WAS WRONG OF ME TO LIE, AND I'D LIKE TO MAKE IT UP TO YOU. I KNOW YOU DON'T TRUST ME RIGHT NOW...
NOT AS FAR AS I COULD THROW YOU.
SO I'VE MADE AN APPOINTMENT AT REALM SPACE WHERE THEY WILL BEAR WITNES TO UNDOING THE CURSE THEY AGREE THAT I FUCKED UP BIG TIME.

DID THEY YELL AT YOU?
YES.
SLURP
FINE.
CLINK
GREAT.
WHEN?
TOMORROW? 5PM?
OK.

ALRIGHT, I'LL LEAVE YOU TO IT.
LIV...
...I LIKE THE SONG YOU PICKED-- FOR YOUR APOLOGY.
I MISSED YOU, TOO.

REALMS
WELCOME BACK!
WINTER AND JAYDE WILL BE ASSISTING ME TODAY TO MAKE SURE THIS ALL GOES ACCORDING TO PLAN.
THANK YOU SO MUCH FOR HELPING ME.
CAN'T
TO
JUST TO BE CLEAR... LIV--?
GREAT.
WILL *NOT* BE PARTICIPATING EXCEPT FOR A FEW NECESSARY PARTS... SINCE SHE CAST THE CURSE.
CAN'T
TO
RUDE.
DON'T EVEN.
SHALL WE GET STARTED?

IT'S OVER NOW, ASH.
CAN'T WAIT TO DIE
HOW DO YOU FEEL?
THE SAME.
BUT LET'S SEE IF IT WORKED!
CAN'T WAIT TO DIE
NO!
RELAX, I'M JUST GOING TO MAKE A SMALL CUT TO SEE IF I STILL REGENERATE.
OH. SORRY.
CAN'T WAIT TO DIE

SO FAR SO GOOD.
NO. NO. NO. NO.
NOOOOOOOOOOOOOOOO.

WHAT DID YOU DO?
CAN'T ... TO DI...
NOTHING! I DID EVERYTHING RIGHT! *RIGHT?*
IF LIV WAS THE ONE WHO CAST THIS SPELL, IT WOULD'VE BEEN UNDONE. SO...
WHAT DO YOU MEAN *IF* LIV CAST THE SPELL? WHO ELSE WOULD IT BE?
CAN'T WAIT TO DIE
DO YOU HAVE ANY OTHER WITCHES IN YOUR LIFE WHO WOULD DO THIS?

UM, NO. MY FAMILY IS *JEWISH.*
IS THERE SOMETHING WE COULD'VE MISSED? DID SOMETHING GET KNOCKED OVER?
WHAT'S THIS?
AN'T WA
TO DI
JUST RESEARCH.
RESEARCH ON SOMNIA? WHAT DOES THAT HAVE TO DO WITH WITCHCRAFT?

dangerous magic
powerful wizard
Greg Caddel?
WHAT DO YOU KNOW ABOUT GREG CADDEL?
I REALLY CAN'T SAY.
HE'S MY MOM'S BOYFRIEND.

HOW DO YOU GUYS KNOW GREG?
HOW DO YOU GUYS KNOW GREG?
LOOK, I CAN'T GIVE YOU DETAILS, BUT I THINK WE MAY HAVE FOUND OUR SUSPECT.
ARE YOU SAYING GREG PRACTICES WITCHCRAFT?
I'M SAYING, IF HE WERE TO HAVE A MOTIVE... MAYBE FIND SOME EVIDENCE IF YOU CAN. *SAFELY.*

SO GREG'S, LIKE, BIG TIME EVIL. NOT JUST ANNOYING MOM BOYFRIEND EVIL.
I GUESS SO.
WHAT DO WE DO?
I HAVE NO FUCKING IDEA.
OOOUUUIIIOOOUUUIII
AMBULANCE
EMMA.

THANK YOU SO MUCH FOR MEETING US.
ARE YOU KIDDING? YOU SAVED MY LIFE. I OWE YOU.
WELL, IT'S FUNNY YOU SAY THAT BECAUSE WE DO HAVE A FAVOR TO ASK.
OK, SHOOT.
WELL. WOULD YOU BE OPEN TO-- JUST ONCE MORE, UM...
CAN YOU GO SEE DR. GREG FOR ONE MORE SESSION, SO WE CAN SNEAK INTO HIS OFFICE AND LOOK FOR EVIDENCE?

WHAT?! I'M JUST TELLING HER THE TRUTH!
I'M SO SORRY ABOUT HER--
SURE.
YOU'LL DO IT?
YEAH, WHY NOT?
I'VE BEEN SEEING A NEW PSYCHIATRIST, ANYWAY. SHE'S MADE ME REALIZE HOW HELPFUL THE RIGHT PERSON--AND MEDICATIONS--CAN BE. DR. GREG WAS BASICALLY THE OPPOSITE OF THAT. HE NEVER REALLY LISTENED TO MY NEEDS.
COOL. THANKS, EMMA.
WHAT'S THE EVIDENCE FOR?
THAT'S CLASSIFIED.

ONCE WE CAN TELL YOU MORE, WE WILL.
SOUNDS GOOD. LIKE I SAID, I OWE YOU. PLUS, I'M TRYING TO GET INTO THE DRAMA PROGRAM AT SCHOOL--SO I NEED SCENE PRACTICE, ANYWAY.
PERFECT.
CAN'T WAIT TO DIE
IF YOU COULD JUST SCHEDULE THE APPOINTMENT FOR--
TOMORROW? DONE.

RIGHT ON TIME.
I MEAN, WE LITERALLY SENT THE UBER. BUT, YEAH, "RIGHT ON TIME."
LET'S GO.

BZZZZZZ
ding
1:42 PM
Emma & Liv
going in.
AND SO ARE WE.

FUCK.
WHAT?
I DON'T KNOW WHICH DOOR.
YOU'VE NEVER BEEN HERE?
NO, I'VE MADE IT MY MISSION TO AVOID THIS OFFICE.
I CAN'T HEAR ANYTHING.
ME EITHER.
We can't figure out which door. Make noise?

I HATE MY LIFE! I HATE EVERYTHING!
DUDE, COME ON!
SHE'S OUR FRIEND. WE SHOULD HELP HER-- WHY DIDN'T SHE TELL US--
SHE'S ACTING!
OH, RIGHT. WOW, SHE'S GOOD.
I'M JUST A GIRL... INTERRUPTED.
SEE?

WHERE DO WE START?
DESK?
LOCKED.
YOU KNOW HOW TO PICK LOCKS? BADASS.
I HATE FEELING LOCKED OUT OF THINGS.
THAT'S PROBABLY SOMETHING YOU SHOULD TELL A THERAPIST.

YES!
SOMNIA
A
ding
1:42
Emma & As
E
going in.
We can't figure
which door. make s
noise?
E
finishing up.
get out.
ASH

LET'S GO.
THANKS FOR SEEING ME ON SUCH SHORT NOTICE, DR. GREG, I--

...I DON'T KNOW WHAT I WAS THINKING TRYING TO SEE A DIFFERENT THERAPIST.
DON'T WORRY, EVERYONE MAKES MISTAKES.
NARCISSIST.
SLAM
RUN.

SORRY--PERIOD. WE HAD TO RUN--PERIOD. WAS HE SUSPICIOUS--QUESTION MARK?
ding
I think you're good. He didn't seem to notice? Did you get everything you need?
I METAL
More than enough. Thank you! Great acting btw. Liv believed you.

LATER.

SO THIS IS...
A LOT MORE WORK THAN WE THOUGHT.
YEAH.
LOTS OF READING...
WAIT--

I STOLE ADDERALL FROM DR. GREG!
YOU STOLE ADDERALL?
IT'S EXPENSIVE! HE DOESN'T NEED IT. HE RUNS ON THE POWERS OF EVIL.
I LOVE YOU AND YOUR WEIRD INCONSISTENCIES.
I LOVE YOU, TOO.

I ALSO STOLE SOMETHING.
WINE?
MUST'VE BEEN A GIFT FROM A PATIENT OR SOMETHING? IT WAS JUST SITTING ON A SHELF.
I'VE NEVER HEARD OF THIS BRAND. "IN VINO VERITAS"? IS IT A NATURAL WINE? I'VE NEVER SEEN BLUE WINE BEFORE.
I DUNNO, BUT IT MUST BE NICE IF HE WAS SAVING IT.
I THOUGHT IT WOULD MAKE STUDYING FEEL MORE FESTIVE.
AND NOW...WE WAIT.

30 MINUTES LATER.
MY ROOM IS SO MESSY-- WOULD YOU MIND IF I CLEANED WHILE WE WAIT?
I THINK IT'S TIME TO GET TO WORK.

MY BRAIN FEELS LIKE SOUP.
FAILURE SOUP. WE DIDN'T EVEN FIND ANYTHING USEFUL. JUST BROKE A BUNCH OF *HIPAA* VIOLATIONS.
I DON'T REMEMBER THIS GROUP OF DOCUMENTS-- ARE THERE OTHERS USING THIS...SHINY PAPER?

IT'S JUST PATIENT NOTES.
I DON'T THINK SO.
WHAT DO YOU MEAN?
IT LOOKS LIKE PATIENT NOTES BUT...I DON'T THINK IT IS.
DO YOU THINK IT'S WRITTEN IN CODE OR SOMETHING?

I'M GOING TO TRY SOMETHING.
HAVE YOU EVER DONE A "WHAT'S IN YOUR BAG"? BECAUSE THIS IS A...HUMAN TOOTH?
I REMEMBER THIS SPELL!
NO WAY! THE LAST TIME YOU CAST A SPELL WAS WHAT GOT US HERE IN THE FIRST PLACE. LET'S JUST GO BACK TO THE SHOP AND--
I'VE GOT THIS. TRUST ME.

IT'S SATURDAY, RIGHT?
RIGHT...
GREAT.
WHY IS THAT GREAT?
SATURDAY IS IN CORRESPONDENCE WITH SATURN.
AND?
SATURN LENDS ITSELF TO KARMA AND JUSTICE. WHICH IS PERFECT FOR WHAT WE'RE DOING.
WILL YOU HOLD MY HAND? IT'LL BE MORE POWERFUL IF YOU HOLD MY HAND.
WHAT WILL BE MORE POWERFUL? I DON'T KNOW IF I WANT YOU TO BE MORE POWERFUL.
JUST LISTEN TO ME! PLEASE!

I GUESS IT CAN'T GET ANY WORSE. YOU CAN'T IMMORTALIZE ME TWICE, RIGHT?
DON'T THINK SO.
YOU DON'T *THINK* SO?
RELAX. JUST CLOSE YOUR EYES AND CONCENTRATE ON REVEALING THE TRUTH OF THIS PAGE, OK?

LET ME SEE WHERE I AM BLIND. LET THE SEAL OF MY THIRD EYE UNWIND.
SEPARATE THE TRUTH AND LIES. SHOW THEM TO ME IN MY EYES.
WELL? DID IT WORK?
IT LOOKS THE SAME JUST...LESS MAGICAL.

THAT'S OK. NOT THE WORST OUTCOME. WANT TO FINISH UP THE WINE AND CALL IT A NIGHT?
YEAH, I GUESS.
OOPH-- SHRIMPS!
CRAP!
HURRY! GET A TOWEL OR SOMETHING--

WAIT.
WHAT?
"IN VINO VERITAS." DUH!
WHAT?
IT'S LATIN FOR "IN WINE, THERE IS TRUTH." THIS WINE IS BASICALLY A WITCHY TRUTH SERUM. LOOK!

SPILL MORE OF IT! GET WINE ON EVERY PAGE!
SOMNIA
SOMNIA
SOMNIA
SOMNIA
SOMNIA
THESE ARE ALL DOCUMENTS ON SOMNIA.
THE PAGES HAD A PROTECTIVE SPELL OVER THEM. MAKES SENSE CONSIDERING YOUR STEP-DAD IS BASICALLY AN EVIL WARLOCK.
HE IS NOT MY STEP-DAD-- HE IS MY MOM'S SHITTY BOYFRIEND. YOU'VE GOTTA STOP MANIFESTING A NEW ROLE FOR HIM IN MY LIFE.

SO... BASICALLY WHAT THIS IS SAYING IS...
WHEN YOU TAKE SOMNIA, YOU'RE NOT JUST TAKING MEDICATION. IT'S BASICALLY A SUPER CONCENTRATED VERSION OF XANAX WITH OTHER INGREDIENTS THAT ADD UP TO A HYPNOSIS SERUM.
SO?
IT MEANS DR. GREG ISN'T TREATING HIS PATIENTS. HE'S HYPNOTIZING THEM AGAINST THEIR WILL AND SLOWING THEM DOWN WITH BENZOS.
SOMNIA
SO...WE GOT HIM! WE TOTALLY GOT HIM! LET'S GO TELL EVERYONE!
ASH. WE CAN'T JUST GO TELL EVERYONE. WE WILL LOOK CRAZY.
BUT WE HAVE PROOF.

SLAM
WHAT TIME IS IT?
SIX.
CANDY CANDY
SHIT! THEY'RE HOME. THEY'RE HOME. I DIDN'T LOOK AT THE TIME--
DON'T WORRY, IT'LL BE OK--THEY STILL HAVE TO COOK DINNER, RIGHT?
ASH! WE'RE HOME! DOES TAKEOUT SOUND OK?

ASH?
HI, ELISE! SORRY, ASH IS JUST FINISHING UP AN ASSIGNMENT--AND SHE'S SUPER IN THE ZONE. IS IT COOL IF I STAY FOR DINNER?
IS THAT LIV? OF COURSE YOU CAN, HONEY.
HIDE THE ADDERALL BOTTLE! WHERE DID IT GO?
KNOCK KNOCK KNOCK

COMING!
RATTLE RATTLE
YOU SAID, "COME IN," RIGHT?
I SAID, "COMING." IT'S RUDE TO ENTER A YOUNG LADY'S ROOM WITHOUT PERMISSION. CAN YOU LEAVE?
YOUR MOM IS IN THE BASEMENT FINISHING UP THE LAUNDRY--SHE SENT ME TO ASK IF CHINESE FOOD SOUNDS OK.
SOUNDS GREAT!

GOOD, I'LL PLACE THE ORDER THEN.
ROLL
ROLL
RATTLE
SONIC

WHAT'S THIS?
WELL?
UHHH, LOOKS LIKE A PRESCRIPTION BOTTLE.
AREN'T YOU SUPPOSED TO BE A DOCTOR? MAYBE BRUSH UP ON THE BASICS, DUDE.
ASH, HAVE YOU BEEN TAKING THESE?
WHAT? NO. WHAT? I'VE NEVER SEEN THOSE BEFORE.
AREN'T THEY YOURS?

STOP PLAYING AROUND, ASH. YOU KNOW *SSRIS* NEED TO BE TAKEN CONSISTENTLY--YOUR TREATMENT PLAN IS NO EXCEPTION.
OH. THOSE! *THOSE.* YES. I'VE BEEN TAKING THOSE. OF COURSE.
THANKS--
I'D SAY I CAUGHT YOU RED-HANDED BUT THAT WOULDN'T BE COMPLETELY ACCURATE, WOULD IT?

WHAT ARE YOU TALKING ABOUT?
GET YOUR HANDS OFF ME.
CAN I SEE BOTH HANDS PLEASE?
OK?
BOTH HANDS AT ONCE PLEASE.

LET GO OF ME!
SHOW ME YOUR OTHER HAND, AND I'LL LET GO.
WELL?

ELLIOTT SMITH
RUN, LIV!
ELLIOTT SMITH
HEY!
YOU RUINED MY RARE ELLIOTT SMITH POSTER, YOU DICK!

HEY! STOP CHASING HER!
HE'S CHASING A MINOR!
SERIOUSLY?
YOU ALL NEED TO GOOGLE KITTY GENOVESE! YOU COULD HAVE BLOOD ON YOUR HANDS!

WELL, FOR ONCE, MY IMMORTALITY IS GOING TO WORK IN MY FAVOR.
I'M SORRY! EMERGENCY!
ASH! STOP!

HEY! YOU CAN'T DRIVE LIKE THAT-- ARE YOU CRAZY? YOU JUST HIT MY KID!
ARE YOU OK?
I'M NOT YOUR KID.
AND I'M FINE.

REC
CLOSED
YOU'RE TOO LATE. THEY'RE CLOSED. WE WON! LATENESS DOESN'T FLY IN WITCH WORLD.

NOBODY WON, ASH. YOU JUST CAUSED A WHOLE LOT OF DAMAGE.
YEAH, DAMAGE TO YOU, LOSER.
DAMAGE TO ME, TO YOU, TO YOUR MOM, TO LOTS OF PEOPLE YOU DON'T EVEN KNOW.
WHAT ARE YOU TALKING ABOUT?
WE WERE HELPING PEOPLE, ASH. WE WERE TRYING TO HELP PEOPLE.
YOU WERE HYPNOTIZING PEOPLE.

DID YOU EVER STOP TO THINK ABOUT WHO WE WERE HYPNOTIZING AND WHY?
UM. YOUR PATIENTS.
BINGO! MY DANGEROUSLY DEPRESSED PATIENTS, YES.
THAT DOESN'T MAKE IT OK, YOU KNOW? YOU CAN'T JUST HYPNOTIZE PEOPLE AND MAKE CHOICES FOR THEM. WE HAVE AUTONOMY. IT'S A HUMAN RIGHT!
COULDN'T YOU ARGUE THAT THE DEPRESSION IS HYPNOTIZING THEM? AND I'M MERELY SERVING UP AN ANTIDOTE TO GET THEM TO THE OTHER SIDE?
IT'S NOT UP TO YOU. YOU'RE NOT GOD AND--MORE IMPORTANTLY--THEY DIDN'T AGREE TO IT!

THEY CONSENTED TO TREATMENT. THEY WANT TO GET BETTER.
YOU'RE NOT MAKING THEM BETTER--YOU'RE IMPRISONING THEM! YOU'RE PUTTING THEM IN BRAIN JAIL!
SOMETIMES, THAT'S WHAT PEOPLE NEED.
THINK OF YOUR FATHER.
DON'T YOU DARE.
IF HE HAD A LITTLE BIT OF WIGGLE ROOM, A LITTLE BIT OF... "BRAIN JAIL," HE MAY STILL BE HERE TODAY.
OH, AND YOU WANT THAT? YOU WOULDN'T BE WITH MY MOM IF MY DAD WAS STILL HERE. DON'T FEIGN KINDNESS TO ME, ASSHOLE.
I WOULD WANT HIM TO STILL BE HERE, YES. I LOVE YOUR MOTHER, AND I WISH I COULD TAKE THAT PAIN AWAY MORE THAN ANYTHING.
BULLSHIT.
IT'S TRUE.

SO YOUR PLAN WAS TO, WHAT--SAVE EVERY SUICIDAL PERSON ON EARTH? THAT'S ACHIEVABLE.
MOSTLY I JUST WANTED TO SAVE YOU.
WELL, KEEP DREAMING...BECAUSE I'M NOT TAKING YOUR FUCKING ZOMBIE PILLS.
I WAS MADE VERY AWARE OF THAT, YES. BUT I'M STILL GOING TO TRY TO PROTECT YOU.
"PROTECT ME"?! HA! YOU JUST WANT TO CONTROL ME. IF YOU WERE SO CONCERNED ABOUT MY HEALTH, WHY DID YOU LET ME GET HIT BY A CAR?
I WOULD'VE STOPPED RUNNING IF YOU STOPPED CHASING MY BEST FRIEND--A TEENAGE GIRL, BY THE WAY.
INSTEAD, I ALMOST BECAME ROADKILL VIA TOYOTA CAMRY. FULLY DEAD ON THE STREETS OF BROOKLYN.
WE BOTH KNOW THAT WASN'T GOING TO HAPPEN.

YOU.
YOU?!
YOU!
YOU DID THIS TO ME? YOU DID THIS TO ME!
YOU'RE A MONSTER. WHAT IS WRONG WITH YOU?
CLOSED
HELP! HELP ME! LET ME IN!

LET ME EXPLAIN.
STAY AWAY FROM ME!
YOUR MOTHER WOULDN'T SURVIVE YOUR DEATH, ASH. SHE JUST WOULDN'T. I'M SAVING HER LIFE.
OH, BY CONTROLLING MINE? OW.
WHAT IN THE WORLD?
HE'S EVIL! HE'S THE ONE! HE CURSED ME!
WHY ARE YOU LETTING HIM IN? HE'S DANGEROUS!
HARDLY. I JUST WANT TO TALK.

THANKS.
WHY ARE YOU HELPING HIM? HE'S YOUR SUSPECT! *YOUR WORDS.* ACTUALLY, SCRATCH THAT, HE'S NOT A SUSPECT ANYMORE-- *HE'S GUILTY!*
DID LIV SHOW YOU THE PAPERS? LIV, DID YOU SHOW THEM THE PAPERS?
I JUST--
IT'S A LITTLE MORE COMPLICATED THAN WE THOUGHT.
HOW IS IT COMPLICATED? YOU WERE LOOKING FOR WHO MADE THIS CREEPY ZOMBIE DRUG.
DR. GREG WAS A SUSPECT. WE HAVE EVIDENCE HE'S GUILTY. THE END.
DR. GREG ALREADY CAME CLEAN TO US.

WHAT?!
DID YOU KNOW ABOUT THIS?
I JUST FOUND OUT.
OK--SO WHAT? HE TELLS YOU THE TRUTH AND GETS OFF SCOT-FREE? THIS IS REAL LIFE, NOT AN AFTERSCHOOL SPECIAL. HE DESERVES PUNISHMENT!
HE CAME TO US TO HELP UNDO THE MAGICAL BIND THAT SOMNIA HAD OVER HIS PATIENTS, AND...
I'M CLOSING MY PRACTICE. IF I CAN'T SEPARATE MY PATIENTS FROM MY PERSONAL AGENDA, I SHOULDN'T BE A PRACTICING DOCTOR.
HE'S LYING! HE JUST SAW A FRIEND OF OURS AS A *PATIENT.*
SHE'S AN *EX-PATIENT,* WHO WAS CLEARLY HAVING SOME SORT OF BREAKDOWN. I FORWARDED HER INFORMATION TO MY COLLEAGUE RIGHT AFTER SHE LEFT.

AND THAT MEANS HE'S ALLOWED TO GET AWAY WITH IT ALL? PEOPLE COULD'VE BEEN SERIOUSLY HURT!
I CAN SEE I WAS WRONG, ASH. AND I'M SORRY. I'M WORKING ON MAKING AMENDS AND REPARATIONS WITH THE COMMUNITY--WITH DYLAN.
TRAITOR!
ASH, IN THE END, NOBODY WAS HARMED, AND THE PROBLEM IS SOLVED.
ACTUALLY, THAT'S NOT TRUE. BECAUSE I'M STILL *CURSED*. CAN YOU GUESS WHAT POWERFUL WIZARD WAS ABLE TO DO THAT? CAUSE IT WASN'T LIV!
IT WAS YOU?
I DIDN'T KNOW WHAT ELSE TO DO.
YEP, SO HE RESORTED TO *HEXING A MINOR.*

YOU'RE JUST A CHILD--YOU CAN'T MAKE THESE KIND OF DECISIONS ON YOUR OWN.
CLASSIC, A MAN TRYING TO CONTROL A WOMAN'S RIGHT TO CHOOSE.
OH, GIVE ME A BREAK. I WAS SAVING YOUR LIFE.
IS THAT SHAKY REASONING HOW YOU'VE BEEN SLEEPING AT NIGHT?
THAT, AND A LOW DOSE OF AMBIEN, YES.
GREG, YOU MUST REMOVE THAT SPELL IMMEDIATELY. YOU KNOW THAT'S NOT RIGHT.
YEAH, NO SHIT.
ONCE WE'RE HOME, I'LL REMOVE IT.

NO CHANCE. REMOVE IT *NOW.*
AND RISK YOU RUNNING INTO TRAFFIC AGAIN? PLUS, THE MATERIALS I NEED ARE AT HOME. I HAVE TO USE THE SAME COMPONENTS I USED THE FIRST TIME TO UNDO THE SPELL.
YOU MEAN *CURSE. YOU. CURSED. ME.*
LET'S GO.
NOT WITHOUT LIV.
LIV IS MORE THAN WELCOME TO JOIN.
SO...THAT'S IT? YOU'RE JUST GOING TO LET ME LEAVE WITH THIS MAN?
IF THERE ARE ANY ISSUES, YOU CAN COME TO ME. BUT I HAVE A FEELING THERE WON'T BE.
IT'S OVER, ASH. I'VE STEPPED AWAY FROM MY MEDICAL PRACTICE. AND NO ONE WILL LISTEN IF YOU--OR ANY OF US--GO SHOUTING ABOUT *MAGIC DRUGS.* LET'S GO HOME. I'LL UNDO THE SPELL.
WHAT'S THE WORST THING THAT CAN HAPPEN? I KILL YOU?
HILARIOUS.

THIS IS SO MESSED UP.
YUP.
MY MOM IS SO BREAKING UP WITH YOU.
SHE IS? WHAT DID SHE SAY?
I MEAN, WHEN I TELL HER WHAT YOU DID!
YOU'RE NOT GOING TO DO THAT.
UH. YEAH, I AM.
NOT IF YOU WANT YOUR CURSE BROKEN.
SO YOU ADMIT IT'S A CURSE!

YOUR MOM DOESN'T BELIEVE IN WITCHCRAFT.
YEAH, WELL, SHE BELIEVES ME. DO YOU REALLY THINK YOU CAN GET AWAY WITH THIS?

LISTEN. I MAY HAVE MESSED UP. BUT I CARE FOR YOUR MOTHER, AND I LOVE HER A LOT. NO OFFENSE, BUT IF YOUR BIG REVEAL IS THAT I GOT YOU TO STAY ALIVE, I DON'T THINK SHE'S GOING TO TURN AGAINST ME, NO MATTER HOW I DID IT.

THE CHOICE IS YOURS. LIFT THE SPELL--
CURSE.
OR DON'T. FINAL OFFER, KIDDO.
THE *CONDESCENSION*-- AFTER EVERYTHING. CAN YOU BELIEVE THIS GUY?
WELL, I DON'T REALLY HAVE A CHOICE, DO I?
GLAD WE CAME TO AN AGREEMENT.
HEY! WAIT--WHEN ARE YOU GOING TO UNDO THE SPELL?
AFTER YOUR MOM GOES TO BED.

HOW DO I KNOW YOU'LL HOLD UP YOUR END OF THE DEAL?
IT'S NOT LIKE I CAN GET AWAY WITH ANYTHING. I'M ALWAYS AROUND.
UGH. RIGHT. AROUND ME.
I'M STARVING.
ME, TOO.
LIV!
WHAT?
I DON'T KNOW--JUST DON'T TALK TO HIM.
I PLACED THE ORDER, BUT THE TAKE OUT PLACE WAS CLOSED! SOME SORT OF HOLIDAY. SORRY, HONEY.
LOOK AT HOW *EASILY* HE *LIES.* SOCIOPATH.

NO WORRIES, I'LL JUST WHIP UP SOMETHING HERE. WE HAVE LEFTOVER LATKES.
YES!
OK, YEAH--THAT DOES SOUND GOOD.
I CAN'T WAIT TO BE ABLE TO DIE AGAIN.
WHAT HONEY?
NOTHING!
CLINK CLINK
SO... HOW WAS EVERYONE'S DAY?

I DON'T HAVE A GOOD FEELING ABOUT THIS--AT ALL.
ASH, HE HAS TO UNDO THE CURSE. YOU HAVE JUST AS MUCH ON HIM AS HE HAS ON YOU.
THAT'S WHAT HE WANTS ME TO THINK.
HE'S A LIAR, DUDE. HE'S MANIPULATIVE, RIGHT?
ABSOLUTELY. AND WE WILL BE ADDRESSING THAT BUT...ONE FOOT IN FRONT OF THE OTHER, RIGHT?
I JUST DON'T TRUST HIM. HE'S NOT A GOOD GUY.
DEFINITELY NOT. BUT WE'LL FIGURE IT OUT. I PROMISE.
KNOCK KNOCK

OH, SO NOW HE LEARNS TO KNOCK. NICE VIRTUE SIGNALING, BRO.
KNOCK KNOCK
THAT'S IT? YOU DON'T NEED MORE... STUFF?
YEP. JUST TAKE A SEAT.
LIV, YOU TOO.
WHY DOES SHE HAVE TO SIT?
I DON'T NEED ANY MISCELLANEOUS MAGIC HAPPENING--I HAVE TO CONCENTRATE. AND, NO OFFENSE, LIV, BUT YOU'RE NOT THE MOST CONTROLLED WITCH.
FINE. GOD, YOU ARE SO PATRONIZING.

I KNOW THIS ISN'T UNDER THE BEST CIRCUMSTANCES BUT...I LIKE THAT WE'RE DOING THIS TOGETHER. FEELS LIKE WE'RE GETTING CLOSER.
ARE YOU ON DRUGS?
ONLY LEGAL ONES!
GIGGLE
LIV, STOP!
--SORRY.
OK, SO... I NEED YOU BOTH TO PUT THESE ON.
ARE YOU KIDNAPPING US?
DO YOU WANT THE CURSE LIFTED OR NOT? WE HAVE TO DO THIS BEFORE MIDNIGHT.
SINCE WHEN?
ASH, MAYBE LET'S JUST GO AHEAD.
READY?
READY.

LATE NIGHT THINK TANK
YOU WERE MY
SWEETEST
TRAP
SHRINK WRAPPED
SHRINK NOTES

LYING HERE AT THE END OF THE WORLD
FUCKING MAGIC
AND ALL...

THAT'S IT?
THAT'S IT.
HOW DO I KNOW YOU DID IT?
YOU'RE JUST GONNA HAVE TO TRUST ME.
I WOULD HIGHLY RECOMMEND NOT SELF-HARMING IN FRONT OF A PSYCHIATRIST. WE HAVE A DUTY TO REPORT, YOU KNOW?
YOU'RE NOT PRACTICING.
DOESN'T MATTER.

JUST GIVE IT A MINUTE.
GOODNIGHT, GIRLS.
NIGHT.
CRAP. I HAVE TO GET HOME. COME WITH?
ding
NAH, I'M GOOD HERE. GONNA TAKE IN BEING MORTAL AGAIN.
OH, OK. I CAN PROBABLY STAY HERE WITH YOU IF YOU WANT. LET ME JUST--
IT'S FINE! I'M FINE. I PROMISE. NOTHING BAD IS GOING TO HAPPEN.

OK, WELL, IF ANYTHING HAPPENS TO YOU, I'LL KILL YOU.
HERE'S HOPING!
NOT FUNNY.
CALL ME IF YOU NEED ANYTHING.

WELL, WE'RE ALONE AGAIN. BACK TO SQUARE ONE. OR, YOU KNOW, PAGE ONE.
OK, NOT FULLY ALONE--SORRY, SHRIMPS.
MEOW
I PROMISED LIV, NOT TONIGHT.
SO WHAT ELSE CAN I GET INTO?

FORBIDDEN PLANETS ALIGN
DRUNK ON MOONLIGHT
THERE'S A PURITY
IN DRINKING FROM THIS PARTICULAR STREAM
OF CHAOS
THOUGH IT ALL FEELS LIKE A BAD JOKE
WHEN IT'S THE SAME DREAM EVERY NIGHT
I TELL MYSELF STORIES OF MY LIFE
AS I REMEMBER IT NOW
BUT I'M GETTING THE FEELING
THAT THE TRUTH OF IT FADES IN AND OUT
LIKE OLD HEADPHONES WITH A BAD WIRE
TIME OF MY LIFE, THE TIME IN MY LIFE
GLIDING ACROSS
GLACIAL
DULL PINK

NOTHING MAKES YOU REALLY WANNA DIE LIKE NOT BEING ABLE TO SLEEP.
MAY AS WELL START THE DAY.
I HAVEN'T BEEN UP HERE IN FOREVER-- FOR OBVIOUS, UH, TRIGGERING REASONS.
FRICK! OW OW OW.

HEY, IT WORKED. AT LEAST GREG TOLD THE TRUTH ABOUT SOMETHING FOR ONCE.
THIS ISN'T SO BAD.
Incoming Call...
Liv

WHAT THE HELL ARE YOU DOING AWAKE?
IT'S THE WEIRDEST THING--I COULDN'T SLEEP AT ALL.
THAT'S UNLIKE YOU.
RIGHT? WHAT ARE YOU DOING?
I'M ON THE ROOF--*JUST* WATCHING THE SUNRISE. DON'T WORRY.
WAIT, NO WAY. I'M ON THE ROOF, TOO! SUCH A GORGEOUS SKY THIS MORNING, IT'S INSANE.

TRULY BEAUTIFUL. EVEN I CAN'T DENY THAT.
YEAH, I THOUGHT IT WAS GOING TO BE THIS PERFECT PINTEREST MOMENT, AND THEN I TOTALLY ATE SHIT AND FELL ON MY WAY UP. SKINNED MY KNEE SO BAD--IT'S GOREY.
REALLY?
WHICH KNEE?
UHH... THE RIGHT? WHY?
OW!
LIV--CAN YOU STAND UP?
SURE, WHY?

OH MY GOD! HI!
HEY.
IT'S SO WEIRD, I KNOW WE LIVE NEAR EACH OTHER BUT I DIDN'T REALIZE WE COULD SEE EACH OTHER.
THERE YOU WERE...
RIGHT IN FRONT OF ME...
THE WHOLE TIME.
CAN'T ANYTHING BE SENTIMENTAL WITH YOU? FOR ONCE?
NO, NO, IT'S--IT'S COOL.
HEY, ASH?
YEAH?
DO YOU THINK ANYTHING'S GONNA CHANGE NOW THAT THE CURSE IS BROKEN?
LIKE WHAT?
I DON'T KNOW. LIKE WILL WE HANG OUT LESS?
IS THIS YOUR WAY OF ASKING IF I'M PLANNING TO CROAK?
NO... ALTHOUGH YOU CAN TACK THAT QUESTION ON, TOO.

I'M NOT GOING ANYWHERE, LIV. ARE YOU?
NO.
COOL.
COOL.
NOW THAT WE'VE ACKNOWLEDGED YOUR ANXIOUS ATTACHMENT STYLE--WHICH WE CAN UNPACK IN FULL LATER--WANNA WATCH THE REST OF THE SUNRISE WITH ME?
LOOK WHO'S SENTIMENTAL NOW.
SO...I FINISHED THE ELLIOTT SMITH BIOGRAPHY.
AND?
I WISH HE WAS STILL ALIVE.
YEAH. ME, TOO.

WANNA HEAR MY NEW FAVORITE ELLIOTT SONG?
SURE.
"Everybody knows everybody knows, you only live a day, but it's brilliant anyway"
I'M EXHAUSTED.
SAME.
TSSSSSS
OWWWWW. OH MY GOD, DID SOMETHING JUST STING ME? IT BURNS.
THAT CAN'T BE GOOD, CAN IT?

HEY, LIV?
YEAH?
DO YOU EVER THINK THAT DEATH MAY BE A... RELIEF?
HMMM. NO.
IT'S GONNA BE A LOOOOONG LIFE.
HERE'S HOPING.

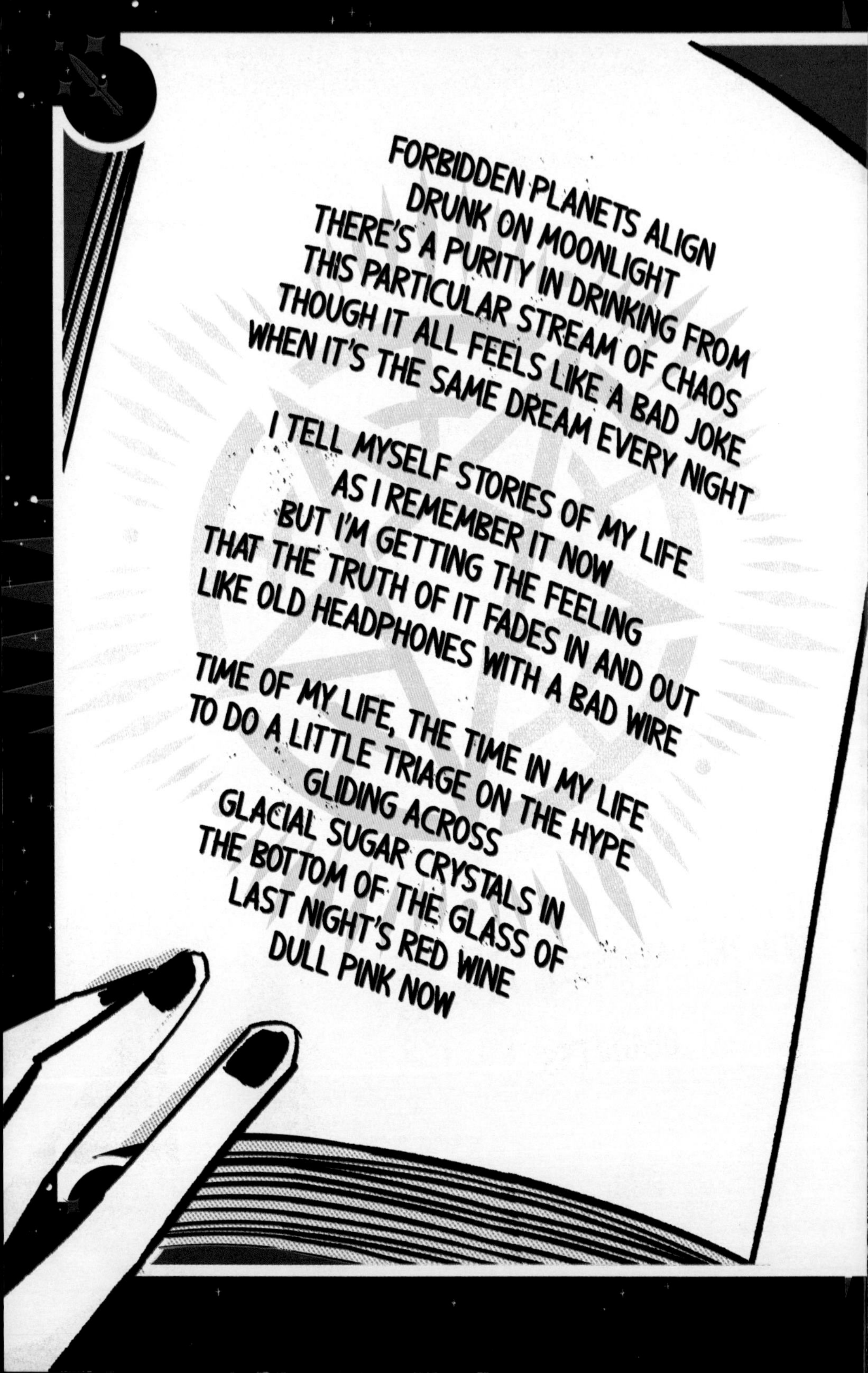
FORBIDDEN PLANETS ALIGN
DRUNK ON MOONLIGHT
THERE'S A PURITY IN DRINKING FROM
THIS PARTICULAR STREAM OF CHAOS
THOUGH IT ALL FEELS LIKE A BAD JOKE
WHEN IT'S THE SAME DREAM EVERY NIGHT
I TELL MYSELF STORIES OF MY LIFE
AS I REMEMBER IT NOW
BUT I'M GETTING THE FEELING
THAT THE TRUTH OF IT FADES IN AND OUT
LIKE OLD HEADPHONES WITH A BAD WIRE
TIME OF MY LIFE, THE TIME IN MY LIFE
TO DO A LITTLE TRIAGE ON THE HYPE
GLIDING ACROSS
GLACIAL SUGAR CRYSTALS IN
THE BOTTOM OF THE GLASS OF
LAST NIGHT'S RED WINE
DULL PINK NOW

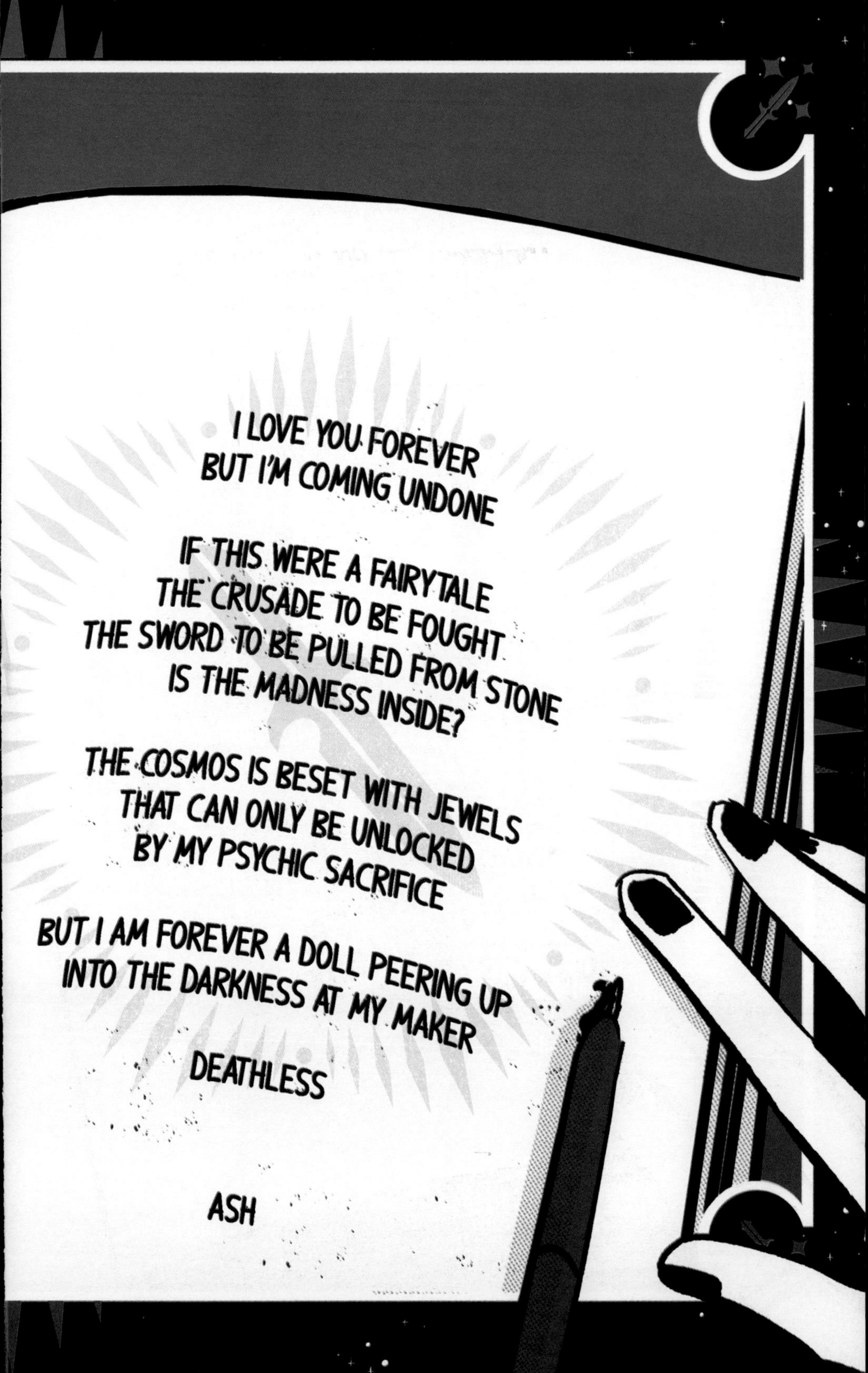
I LOVE YOU FOREVER
BUT I'M COMING UNDONE
IF THIS WERE A FAIRYTALE
THE CRUSADE TO BE FOUGHT
THE SWORD TO BE PULLED FROM STONE
IS THE MADNESS INSIDE?
THE COSMOS IS BESET WITH JEWELS
THAT CAN ONLY BE UNLOCKED
BY MY PSYCHIC SACRIFICE
BUT I AM FOREVER A DOLL PEERING UP
INTO THE DARKNESS AT MY MAKER
DEATHLESS
ASH

PLAYLIST

https://spotify.link/RMsvejjk6Hb

NEEDLE IN THE HAY
bad astronaut

BATH COUNTY
wednesday

SATANIST
boygenius

FILL IN THE BLANK
car seat headrest

KILL ME
indigo de souza

BLED WHITE
elliott smith

HANG ME
tancred

HALF RIGHT
heatmiser

PRETEND
alex_g_offline

SPIT IT OUT
softcult

CHANGE
alex g

LUCKY SMOKE RINGS
mike felumelee/dan andriano

OFF MY MIND
joe p

SCAREDY PANTS
venus & the flytraps

BALLAD OF A HOMESCHOOLED GIRL
oilivia rodrigo

RIOT
daisy grenade

LEAP YEAR
heart attack man

AT YOUR FUNERAL
saves the day

I KNOW WHAT U MEAN
hotline tnt

BE CAREFUL WITH YOURSELF
julia jacklin

PETE ✦ WENTZ

Lyricist and bassist for multi-platinum selling, GRAMMY-nominated rock band Fall Out Boy. He owns the record label DCD2 Records which signed Panic! At The Disco and whose roster currently includes CARR, Daisy Grenade, Games We Play, nothing,nowhere., and more. In addition to music, Wentz created the graphic novel Dying Inside with Hannah Klein and Lisa Sterle for Vault Comics imprint Headshell, launched his own jewelry and apparel line, and is an avid tennis player. Wentz originally hails from Chicago, IL.

HANNAH ✦ KLEIN

Writer/director working in film, music, and (now) graphic novels. She's passionate about mental health, girlhood, and using gossip as a form of currency. She was raised in New York City, where she still resides with her half-hairless cat and the ghost that haunts her apartment.

LISA ✦ STERLE

Columbus artist with work spanning from comic books to concept design to pop-culture-fueled illustration. Her work is often bright, expressive, and occasionally tinged with horror, marrying her two favorite themes: the beautiful and the grotesque. She has worked with HarperCollins, IDW, Image, Archie Comics, Vault Comics, BOOM! Studios, and many others. She is the co-creator of monthly comics Long Lost, Submerged, and Witchblood, as well as the creator of The Modern Witch Tarot Deck, a modern and diverse interpretation of the classic Rider-Waite tarot deck, and the illustrator of the graphic novel Squad with writer Maggie Tokuda-Hall.

end.